Dear Reader,

There is an artist inside every one of us, and it's time to let your inner artist shine! This book is about more than just doodling tattoos on your body—it's also about exploring your creative side. When you draw, you visually express the thoughts, ideas, and dreams that make you unique. Art isn't just something that hangs on a wall, that you need expensive materials to create—it's something you can create right here, right now, using body art markers or tattoo pens, with your body as a canvas. When you doodle tattoos on your body, you're creating a work of art. Yes, it will fade or wash off over time, but that's the beauty of it. You can then begin again with a clean slate and create something totally new and exciting each time!

When you follow the lessons in this book, feel free to change the steps, add your own details, and use any colors you want. Make the designs reflect your personality and interests. Above all, have fun and keep on drawing!

Thaneeya McArdle

Publisher Karen Cooper

Managing Editor, Everything® Series Lisa Laing

Copy Chief Casey Ebert

Assistant Production Editor Alex Guarco

Acquisitions Editor Lisa Laing

Senior Development Editor Brett Palana-Shanahan

Everything® Series Cover Designer Erin Alexander

Visit the entire Everything® series at *www.everything.com*

The EVERYTHING® Girls

50+ cool doodle tattoos to create and wear!

Ultimate Body Art Book

Thaneeya McArdle

Adams media

Avon, Massachusetts

To my mom, for always letting me be me!

An Everything® Series Book.
Everything® and everything.com® are registered trademarks of F+W Media, Inc.

Published by
Adams Media, a division of F+W Media, Inc.
57 Littlefield Street, Avon, MA 02322. U.S.A.
www.adamsmedia.com

ISBN 10: 1-4405-7351-4
ISBN 13: 978-1-4405-7351-4
eISBN 10: 1-4405-7352-2
eISBN 13: 978-1-4405-7352-1

Printed by RR Donnelley, Harrisonburg, VA, U.S.A.

10 9 8 7 6 5 4 3 2 1

June 2014

Interior art by Thaneeya McArdle.
Cover illustrations by Thaneeya McArdle; © blue67/123RF.

This book is available at quantity discounts for bulk purchases.
For information, please call 1-800-289-0963.

Contents

Acknowledgments

Thank you to my husband Marcus, for doing all the dishes while I wrote this book, and also for being a willing body model when I needed to practice doodle tattoo designs. Your love and support means more to me than I can ever say.

Thank you to Pam Wissman for approaching me about this book, and to Lisa Laing, Erin Alexander, and everyone at Adams Media who helped carry this book from concept to completion. Publishing a book is truly a group effort and I couldn't have asked for a better experience.

Introduction

Shooting stars, flying cats, scrumptious cupcakes . . . these are just a few of the super-cool doodle tattoos you'll learn to make in this book! Get ready to explore your creativity while making a fashion statement at the same time.

In this book you'll learn how to draw a wide range of cool images—such as butterfly bracelets, smiling sugar skulls, ice cream sundaes, and so much more! Imagine a fish swimming across your arm, a butterfly dancing above your ankle, a delicate vine of flowers wrapped around your wrist . . . if you can imagine it, you can draw it!

The lessons in this book are designed to sharpen your drawing skills, expand your creativity, and (most importantly) teach you how to draw really cool temporary body tattoos.

The step-by-step lessons in this book are designed to make doodle tattoos fun and easy to create, so no prior drawing skills are needed. If you're unsure where to begin, check out the section on shapes and patterns to help get your creative juices flowing, and open your eyes to a world of tattoo possibilities!

Flip through this book and start with the images that excite you. Some will look easy to create and some might look challenging, but once you practice and follow the steps you'll be creating tattoos that delight and amaze your friends and family! So don't be afraid of images in this book that might look complicated, because each lesson is broken down into easy steps that you can follow from start to finish.

It's best to practice your tattoo ideas on paper first, so you can sharpen your skills and develop your ideas. Use pencils, colored pencils, markers, or crayons for doodling designs. Don't be afraid to experiment—that's what art is all about! Try different colors and patterns. Feel free to deviate from the lessons by adding your own personal twist to design tattoos that are uniquely you!

Once you're ready to draw your designs on your body, remember to always use washable, nontoxic materials that are meant for use on skin. Look for products like body art markers, pens, or crayons; tattoo glitter pens and gel pens; and makeup such as eyebrow or eyeliner pencils. If you're unsure, ask your parents to buy these for you. You'll also need moist towelettes or makeup remover pads (to erase mistakes and for cleanup).

When you're ready to doodle on your skin, make sure the area where you want to draw is clean and dry. Test the marker, crayon, pen, or pencil on a small patch of skin to see if it causes a reaction. Some people have more sensitive skin than others.

Before you start an elaborate doodle, practice with each material first to see what kind of mark it makes. For example, body art crayons tend to be blunt, which is great for covering large spaces with color. Tattoo gel pens have a fine point, so they are excellent for drawing outlines and creating details. The better you know your drawing tools, the more amazing your doodle tattoos will be! For many of the lessons in this book, it's best to use a pencil or pen with a fine point to draw the design. When you're done with the outline you can use markers or crayons to color it in!

You can doodle temporary tattoos anywhere you can safely reach on yourself or your friends—such as hands, fingers, wrists, arms, ankles, legs—any skin area invites self-expression! (Just be sure not to draw near your eyes or mouth.) As you draw, try not to make marks on your clothes, furniture, or the carpet. When you're finished, treat your tattoo like the work of art that it is and be careful not to accidentally rub your tattoo on the couch or the curtains!

Want to add extra sparkle to your designs? These doodle tattoos can be enhanced with fun body art accessories like body glitter, gems, or stencils, which are available at many stores and online. They often come in kits with instructions that explain how to use them. However, these accessories are no substitute for the endless creativity at your fingertips when you pick up a pencil or marker and doodle your own original designs!

Are you ready to doodle, design, and draw your own body art tattoos? Gather your supplies and let's get started!

Chapter 1

Doodle Jewelry

If you're into bling and fashion, turn your passion into art by designing your own body art jewelry tattoos! Learn how to draw an awesome array of rings, bracelets, and necklaces. Deck yourself out in these cool jewelry designs for fingers, wrists, necks— you can even draw armbands and anklets, too!

How to Make Patterns

Patterns can be a really groovy part of your body art designs. For example, you can wrap patterns around your wrists or ankles to make body jewelry, or incorporate patterns into cute images like owls and flowers! Patterns are a great way to "fill space" and instantly make any design look trendy. You'll see patterns all throughout this book, so let's start with a few lessons on how to make your own awesome patterns.

Making patterns is easy and fun. All you do is start with a shape and repeat it! Then you add other repeating shapes to make your design unique.

Basic Shapes

All patterns start with a shape, which can be as simple as a dot or a line. Here are several basic shapes that can form the starting point for your patterns. You're probably already familiar with most of these shapes, but notice how the same shape can look different and have its own personality when you change its size, color, or position.

When drawing a shape, you can make it big or little, skinny or wide. You can draw it upside-down, on its side, or at an angle. Have fun with it! Let loose and see what happens!

Circles and dots

Squares and rectangles

Triangles

Ovals

Raindrops

Stars

Simple flowers

Hearts

Spirals

Half-circles and ovals
(some with pointy tips!)

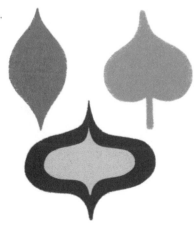

Leaves or petals

TIP: You can also draw shapes inside of shapes to add more pizzazz to your body art tattoos! Try combining different shapes and see what you come up with.

Basic Patterns

Let's get started by looking at some basic patterns to get your creative juices flowing. If making patterns sounds daunting, just note how each of these patterns starts out as a simple line or dot. As the famous artist Paul Klee once said, "A line is a dot that went for a walk." Can you make your line dance, twirl, jump, and play?

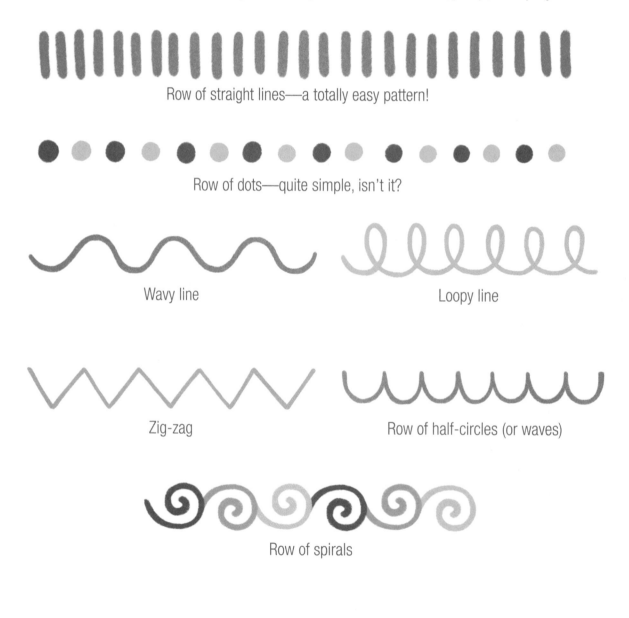

Row of straight lines—a totally easy pattern!

Row of dots—quite simple, isn't it?

Wavy line

Loopy line

Zig-zag

Row of half-circles (or waves)

Row of spirals

Making patterns isn't just about repeating shapes! You can also make patterns with color by repeating a color scheme. Take another look at the row of dots and the row of spirals on the previous page. Can you see how each pattern has its own set of repeating colors? Try it when you doodle—the results will delight you!

Now let's take a small step forward and start creating some super-simple patterns.

Draw a wavy line with another wavy line on top.
Connect them with a row of short straight lines. Easy-peasy!

Step 1: Draw a row of "humps," which are basically half-ovals.
These shapes are perfect for drawing petals!

Step 2: Decorate the petals by adding dots and coloring them in!

Symmetrical Patterns

A fun way to make simple patterns look fancy-schmancy is to make them symmetrical! Symmetry occurs when one half of the design is a mirror image of the other half. This is a fabulous technique to keep in mind when designing your body tattoos—particularly body art jewelry like bracelets and rings!

Here are several examples of symmetrical patterns to spark your creativity:

Loopy line with a flower in the center

Long raindrop shapes with
a heart in the center

Although the flower isn't perfectly
symmetrical, the designs on the left and right
are symmetrical to each other.

Wavy lines with flowers, dots, and leaves

Patterns Step by Step

Now let's make some patterns, step by step! Feel free to follow these instructions as given, or go off on your own creative tangent to give each pattern your own unique spin.

TIP: Don't pressure yourself to make your designs perfectly symmetrical. If each half doesn't match up 100%, that just gives the design some personality!

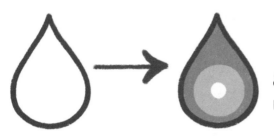

Step 1: Start by drawing a simple raindrop shape, and then color it in.

Step 2: Draw a whole row of repeating raindrop shapes, and put a small circle in between each one.

Step 3: Draw a small heart on top of each raindrop. What a cute pattern!

Here's another fun pattern for you to try:

Step 1: Draw a row of stars.

Step 2: Draw a wavy line that weaves in between each star. You can also decorate the line—see how this line has stripes?

Step 3: Add rows of dots on the tops and bottoms of the wavy line. This pattern looks cool as it is, but you can choose to take it a step further. . . .

Step 4: If you want to make your pattern even more fancy and whimsical, add loopy lines on the tops and bottoms of the waves!

This next pattern looks elegant—and complicated!—but you'll see that it's actually quite easy when you take it one step at a time.

Step 1: Draw a long loopy line, like so.

Step 2: Draw a circle underneath the line, in between the loops.

Step 3: Draw a pointy petal shape in between each loop.

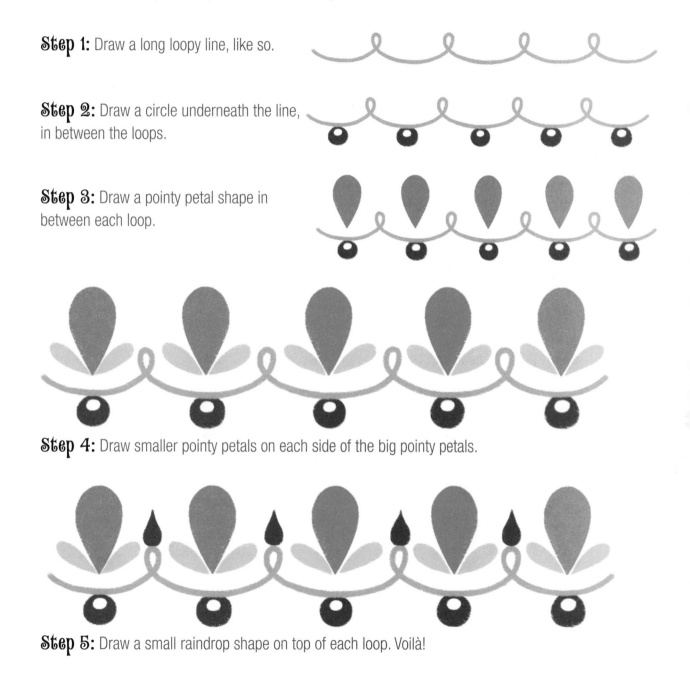

Step 4: Draw smaller pointy petals on each side of the big pointy petals.

Step 5: Draw a small raindrop shape on top of each loop. Voilà!

Now that you know how to make patterns, the sky's the limit! Remember, you can take any shape and repeat it to start your pattern, and then simply add more repeating shapes and colors until your pattern looks finished. You can make your patterns as detailed or as simple as you want, it's up to you!

Rings

Deck out your fingers in these cool doodle rings! Draw them at the base of your finger, in the exact spot where you'd wear a ring. You don't need to stop at just one—you can draw a bunch of rings on several different fingers, and even draw a bunch of rings on the same finger.

When you draw rings, you can make them wrap around your entire finger, or they can just sit on top of your finger. Either way, when drawing rings, it's best to use a fine-tipped marker or pen so you can create more detail.

Flower Ring

Learn how to draw a cute flower ring with spirals on each side.

Step 1: Draw a simple flower, like this one.

Step 2: Add 2 symmetrical swirls, one on each side of the flower.

Step 3: Draw 2 more symmetrical swirls on each side of the flower, facing the opposite direction of the first set of swirls.

Step 4: Add dots.

Step 5: Color it in!

Peace Ring

Time to get groovy with this flowery peace sign ring!

Step 1: Draw a peace sign.

Step 2: Draw a flower around the peace sign.

Step 3: Draw leaves on the sides of the flower.

Step 4: Color it in!

Heart Ring

Let's draw a heart with wings and a halo.

Step 1: Draw a heart.

Step 2: Draw a pair of wings on the heart.

Step 3: Draw a halo above the heart.

Step 4: Add some decorative details to the wings.

Step 5: Color it in!

Bracelets

You can turn any pattern into a cool bracelet just by repeating shapes and colors, so you've already got a head start on making doodle bracelets! Here are a few more lessons to spark your creativity.

You can doodle these bracelets around your wrists, or draw them around your upper arm to make arm bands, or draw them around your ankles to make anklets!

Flower Bracelet

Learn how to draw flowers on a vine that wraps around your wrist—perfect for a nature-lovin' hippie chick!

Step 1: Draw a wavy line.

Step 2: Add flowers to the vine.

Step 3: Add leaves.

Step 4: Add loops, swirls, and dots.

Heart Bracelet

Here's how to draw an elegant heart bracelet.

Step 1: Draw a heart.

Step 2: Add details to the heart by drawing a smaller heart inside the heart, and drawing petals or other shapes around the outside of the heart.

Step 3: Add more detail to the heart and color it in.

Step 4: Draw wavy lines on each side of the heart.

Step 5: Add shapes in between each "hump" of the wave.

Butterfly Bracelet

Follow these steps to create a beautiful butterfly bracelet.

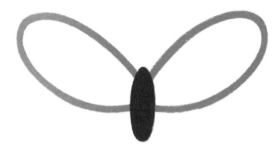

Step 1: Draw the butterfly's body and top pair of wings. Try to make the wings symmetrical.

Step 2: Draw the bottom pair of wings.

Step 3: Add a pair of antennae. Draw some decorative details on the butterfly's wings. If you don't have enough room for adding details, you can just add simple circles to the wings, or you can skip this step.

Step 4: Color in the butterfly.

Step 5: On each side of the butterfly, draw a loopy line with a flower at each end. Try to make each side symmetrical.

Step 6: Color in the flowers and loops.

Step 7: Optional: Draw raindrops (or other shapes) in between each loop.

Necklaces

Doodle necklaces can be elegant or funky, sophisticated or cute! You'll probably find that it's easier to draw necklaces on your friends than it is to draw one on yourself. However, it can still be fun to practice drawing necklaces on yourself in a mirror, and it will sharpen your hand-eye coordination! Remember to draw softly when you doodle necklaces because the neck area is quite sensitive to touch. Also be careful not to stain your shirt when drawing doodle necklaces.

String of Flowers Necklace

This necklace resembles a string of flowers and beads.

This is how the finished necklace will look.

Step 1: Draw a flower at the base of the neck, in the center.

Step 2: Draw flowers on each side of the first flower. Draw them a little higher than the first flower. You can make the flowers symmetrical, like the ones here, or you can make them different. It's up to you!

Step 3: Draw another pair of flowers, a little higher than the previous flowers.

Step 4: Draw a string of beads connecting the flowers. The beads can be dots like the ones here, or you can draw them in other shapes like hearts, stars, triangles, etc.

Step 5: Color it in!

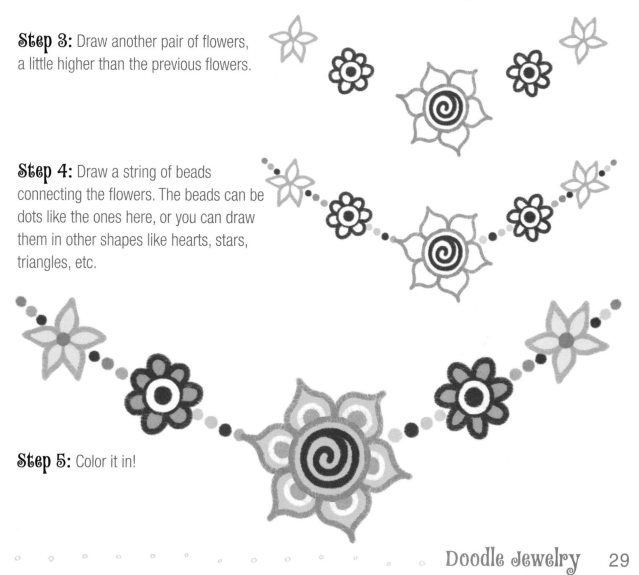

Heart Swirl Necklace

Draw an elegant necklace with swirls spreading out from a heart.

This is how the necklace will look when it's finished.

Step 1: Draw a heart in the center of your neck.

Step 2: On one side of the heart, draw a swirl, like this.

Step 3: Using a different color, draw a connecting swirl going in the opposite direction.

Step 4: Draw another connecting swirl, like so.

Step 5: Keep drawing more swirls until you reach the side of your neck, or if you are drawing on a friend, you can keep going to make the necklace connect at the back.

Step 6: Draw connecting swirls on the opposite side of the heart.

Happy Sunshine Necklace

Here's how to draw a groovy necklace to show off your sunny personality! Feel free to add more details to the sun and use bright colors. Let your inner light shine!

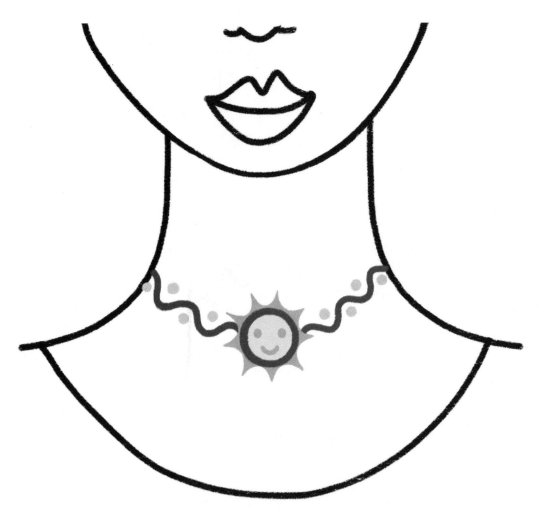

This is how the necklace will look when it's finished.

Step 1: Start by drawing a circle near the lower center of your neck. Draw rays emanating from the circle to make it look like a sun.

Step 2: Give the sun a cute happy face!

Step 3: Draw wavy lines extending from each side of the sun. You can stop the lines at the sides of your neck, or if you're drawing on a friend, continue the lines all the way around so they meet at the back.

Step 4: Add shapes in between each wave, like these circles. You could also add flowers, stars, peace signs, or any other shape you can think of.

Doodle Your Own

Now it's your turn! Here are some basic patterns to get you started. Make these patterns your own patterns by adding repeating shapes in any colors you want!

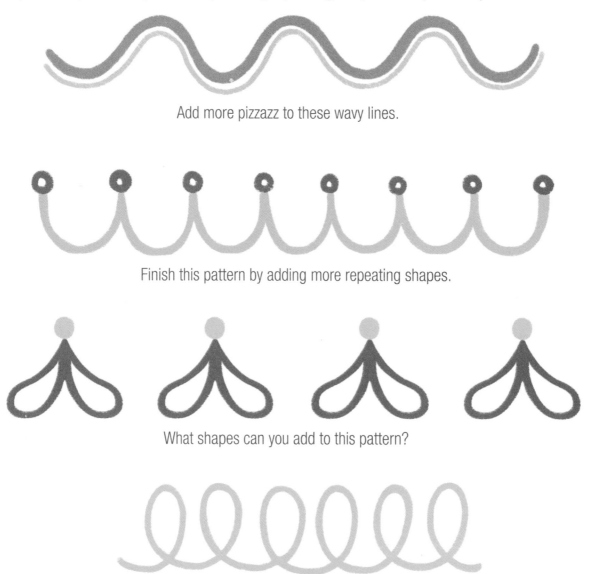

Add more pizzazz to these wavy lines.

Finish this pattern by adding more repeating shapes.

What shapes can you add to this pattern?

Have fun with this loopy line!

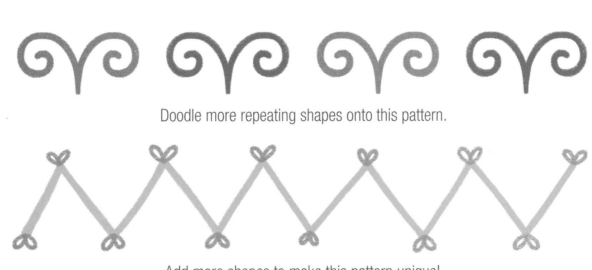

Doodle more repeating shapes onto this pattern.

Add more shapes to make this pattern unique!

Now it's time to get creative and design your own body jewelry! Finish these doodles using pencils, pens, or markers. Add your own creative flair to each piece. Go wild with color and patterns!

Finish this flower necklace by adding more flowers, beads, or anything else you wish.

Add more repeating shapes to this pattern to make a unique necklace!

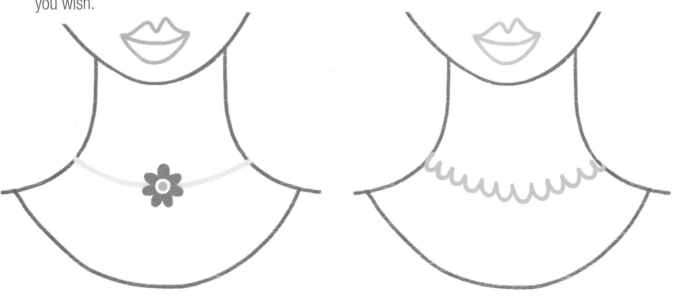

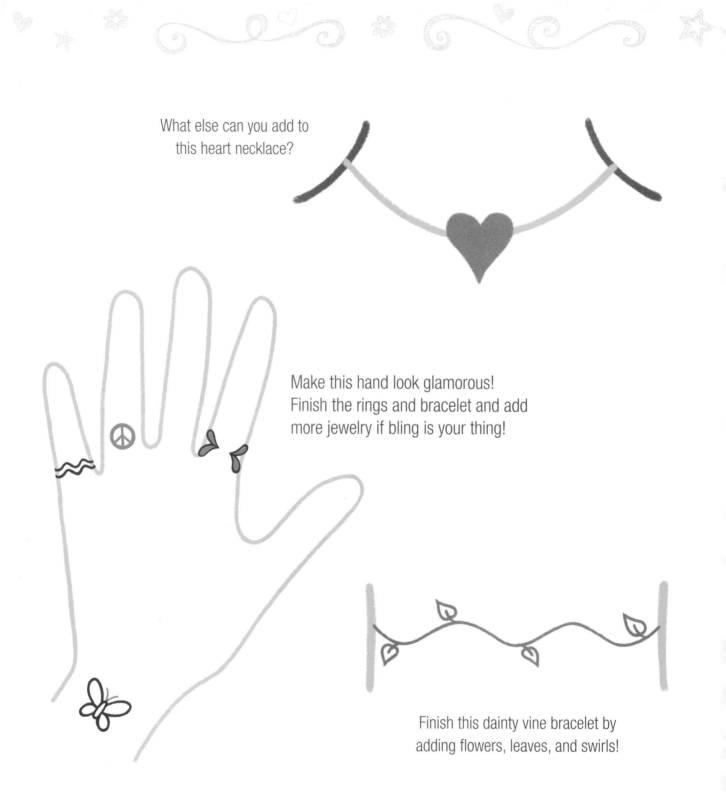

What else can you add to this heart necklace?

Make this hand look glamorous! Finish the rings and bracelet and add more jewelry if bling is your thing!

Finish this dainty vine bracelet by adding flowers, leaves, and swirls!

Chapter 2

Doodle Mini Abstract Tattoos

Learn how to doodle fun abstract designs, such as flowers, starbursts, paisleys, mandalas, and hearts! You have so much room for creativity with these types of images. There are endless possibilities in terms of shapes, colors, and patterns. Follow these steps as a guide, but feel free to substitute your own shapes and patterns whenever you want! Part of the fun of drawing abstract tattoos is that you can draw these images over and over again and they'll look different each time!

Flowers

Flowers look fantastic as body doodles, with lots of opportunities for creative expression. Learn to build up details to create intricate, fascinating flowers that are uniquely you! You can draw these flowers big or small, using one color or lots of colors. The important thing is to have fun with it!

Fancy Flower

Follow these easy steps to draw a fancy flower.

Step 1: Draw a small circle. You can make the circle look more fancy by coloring the inside using another color, and outlining it in a different color.

Step 2: Draw small petals around the outside edge of the circle.

Step 3: Draw large petals.

Step 4: Accent the edges of the petals by coloring them in.

Step 5: Draw small petal shapes inside the big petals.

Step 6: Draw swirls sprouting from between the petals.

Step 7: Add dots. If you want, you can keep adding more decorative details, like loops or petals, until you run out of room!

Pointy Flower

Here's how to draw a pointy flower with a stem and leaves.

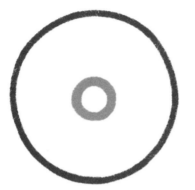

Step 1: Draw two circles, one inside the other.

Step 2: Draw a small flower inside the circle. (You can choose to add other shapes or patterns instead.)

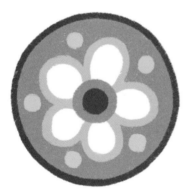

Step 3: Color it in.

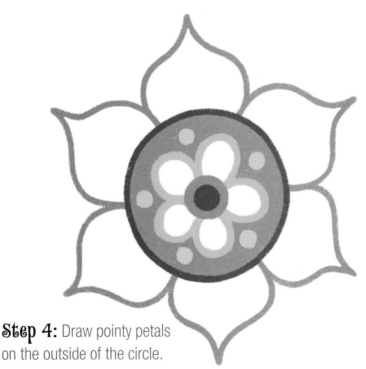

Step 4: Draw pointy petals on the outside of the circle.

Step 5: Add a shape in the center of each petal (like a raindrop or a circle) and color in the petals.

Step 6: Optional: Draw another set of pointy petals behind the petals you just colored in. (This can give the flower a stronger sense of depth.)

Step 7: Draw a stem and leaves.

Chic Flower

This flower has a lot of steps, which show how you can keep adding more designs and details to your flower to make it look ultra chic!

Step 1: Draw circles, one inside another, using different colors.

Step 2: Draw flower petals around the circle, like shown. These petals resemble hearts.

Step 3: Draw raindrop shapes inside the petals, and color them in.

Step 4: Draw a line around the flower that echoes the petal shapes you've already drawn.

Step 5: Draw petals in between each hump.

Step 6: Draw a circle in between each petal.

Step 7: Draw a line that goes around the outside of the flower, and color in this area.

Step 8: Draw a row of small half-circle petals around the outside edge of the flower.

Chic Flower with Leaves

Follow these easy steps to add cute leaves to your flowers!

Step 1: Draw a few leaves connected to your chic flower, so it looks like they are coming out from underneath the flower.

Step 2: Draw a line bisecting each leaf.

Step 3: Add details inside the leaves.

Step 4: Color them in!

Groovy Tulip

This flower doodle is inspired by tulips. Add your own shapes and patterns to the tulip to make it unique!

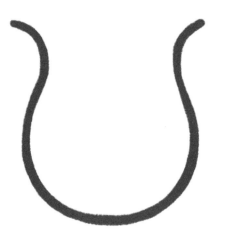

Step 1: Draw a U-shape with the top ends curving outward, like this.

Step 2: At the top of the flower, draw 2 pointy petals on each side.

Step 3: Draw the pointy middle petal like so.

Step 4: Add shapes to the top of the flower, like circles and swirls.

Step 5: Add shapes and patterns to the flower and color it in.

Step 6: Add a stem and leaves.

Starbursts

Reach for the stars with these trendy starburst doodle tattoos! Learn to draw shooting stars that swirl and soar. Fill them with colorful designs!

Swirly Star

Here are the steps for drawing an out-of-this-world swirly shooting star.

Step 1: Draw a star. If you want, you can decorate your star with shapes and designs or color it in with multiple colors.

Step 2: Draw a dot to the upper right of the star. This will be the end point, where the "rays" of the star will emerge.

Step 3: Using a circular motion, draw big swooping lines from the tips and corners of the star to the dot, like shown.

Step 4: Finish connecting the tips and corners with the dot. Note how the line touching the bottom right tip of the star touches the bottom left side of the star and stops. This helps give your drawing a sense of depth. There will also be a couple of corners of the star that you don't need to connect to the dot. Now your star looks like a swirling shooting star!

Step 5: Add to the effect by drawing a swirl from the end of the shooting star.

Step 6: Color it in!

Starburst

This fun, cute starburst features spirals and other shapes radiating into space. Learn how to create this super-cool design in just a few steps!

Step 1: Draw a star on the upper left and color it in. Draw a dot on the bottom right.

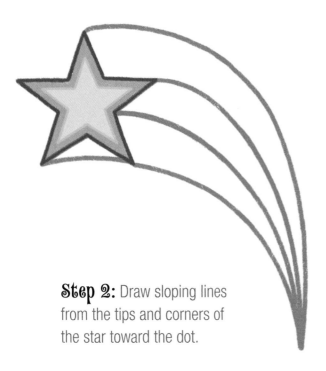

Step 2: Draw sloping lines from the tips and corners of the star toward the dot.

Step 3: Color it in, filling each section with patterns, if you like.

Step 4: Draw spirals on each side of the star's rays, and color them in (you can fill them with patterns if you want).

Step 5: Draw raindrop shapes springing from one of the corners between the star's rays and the spiral. Decorate them with shapes and color them in.

Step 6: Add more spirals, stars, and dots, and color them in. How cool!

Multi-Starbursts

This starburst features three shooting stars. It might look complicated, but if you take it one step at a time, you'll be able to create this groovy starburst that will dazzle your friends! The design is rather large, so make sure you choose a body part that gives you enough room, like an arm or a leg. You might want to use fine-tipped markers or pens to create the outlines and use markers or crayons to color in the designs.

Step 1: Draw 3 stars, and a small dot below, beneath the middle star.

Step 2: Draw lines from the top middle star to the dot at the bottom.

Step 3: Draw gently sloping lines from the tips and corners of the star on the right to the dot below.

Step 4: Draw the rays for the star on the left.

Step 5: Color in the rays. When you use alternating colors like you see here, it helps the starburst look 3-D.

Step 6: Draw swirls at the bottom of the star's rays.

Step 7: Add some swirls, long raindrop shapes, and small stars on each side of the drawing.

Step 8: Add some swirls, dots, and small stars at the top.

Mandalas

Mandalas are like elegant, circular doodles that radiate out from a central point. You can add as much detail as you want to your mandala doodles, which is part of the fun! Follow these steps to create inspiring doodle mandalas, then experiment to create your own unique designs!

Mandala A

When you draw mandalas, you're basically drawing rows of patterns that go around in a circle. Try to use all your favorite patterns when you draw mandalas!

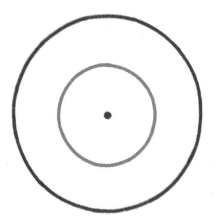

Step 1: Draw a dot, then draw a circle around the dot, and another circle around that.

Step 2: Draw petal shapes coming out from the dot.

Step 3: Draw patterns in between the two circles, such as these pointy petals and dots.

Step 4: Draw petals on the outside edge of the biggest circle.

Step 5: Color it in!

Mandala B

This mandala starts out like the previous one and then adds more "rows" or layers. An easy way to draw mandalas is to start doodling from the center and work your way outward, adding as much detail and color as you like.

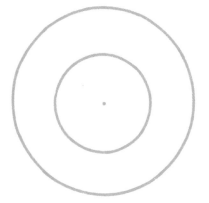

Step 1: Draw a dot, then draw a circle around the dot, and another larger circle around that.

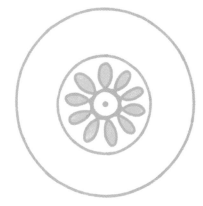

Step 2: Draw a loopy line around the dot and color it in.

Step 3: Add more designs to the next row, such as the designs shown here.

Step 4: Draw raindrop shapes around the outer edge of the largest circle.

Step 5: Color it in!

Mandala 6

Let's draw a mandala that looks like a flower with pointy petals. You can also add a stem and leaves to your mandalas to turn them into funky flowers!

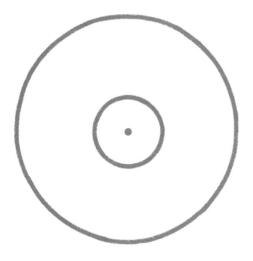

Step 1: Draw a dot with a circle around it, and then draw another circle around that.

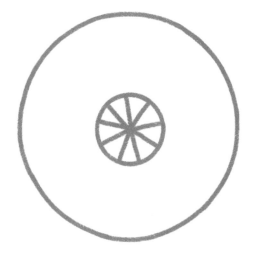

Step 2: Add some designs to the inner circle, such as this row of lines extending outward from the central dot.

Step 3: Draw designs in the outer circle, such as waves and dots as shown here, or anything else you want!

Step 4: Draw shapes and patterns on the outside of the circle, such as this row of pointy petals.

Step 5: Add more shapes to the outer petals, like you see here.

Step 6: Color it in!

Paisley

"Paisley" is a term for a shape that resembles a fat raindrop with a twist, which is then filled with shapes, patterns, and designs. When you draw a lot of paisley shapes next to each other, it looks best if each one is facing a different direction, so in these lessons you'll learn how to draw paisleys in different positions.

Paisley A

Step 1: Start by drawing the small roundish tip of the paisley. Draw a shape that looks like a backward "c," similar to what you see here.

Step 2: Finish the paisley by drawing a large raindrop shape with a bulge that leans to the left.

Step 3: Add shapes in the large part of the paisley, such as these circles with a flower in the center.

Step 4: Add a pattern around the main circle, and a dot or other shape in the small circle at the top of the paisley.

Step 5: Add more shapes and designs, such as raindrops, circles, and anything else you can think of!

Step 6: Add a row of half-circles to the outer edge of the paisley. Your row of half-circles can wrap around the entire paisley or just part of it, as shown here.

Step 7: Color it in!

Paisley B

Step 1: Draw a spiral, like this one. This will be the tip of the paisley.

Step 2: Draw the paisley shape. Make sure to give it a big bulge so you have lots of room to add cool decorations!

Step 3: Draw a long line stretching across near the bottom of the paisley, with short straight lines connecting to the paisley's edge.

Step 4: Draw a row of half-ovals or half-circles on top of the long line you drew in Step 3.

Step 5: Add more decorations like dots, waves, etc.

Step 6: Draw flowers to fill the rest of the paisley.

Step 7: Color it in!

Paisley 6

This paisley has a splashy tail!

Step 1: Draw a shape that looks like a large twisted raindrop on its side. (It also resembles a speech bubble that you'd find in comics!)

Step 2: Draw 3 smaller twisted raindrop shapes that connect to the pointed tip of your large raindrop.

Step 3: In the big bulge of the paisley, draw a curved line that turns that end of the paisley into a circle. Draw a smaller circle in the center of the bigger circle.

Step 4: Draw a flower around the small circle.

Step 5: Add designs to the edge of the circle inside the paisley.

Step 6: Add designs to the "tail" end of the paisley.

Step 7: Add more designs to the paisley, using any shapes or patterns you want!

Step 8: Color it in!

Hearts

Hearts have always been a popular image for body tattoos. Learn how to draw 3 fun types of hearts: an abstract heart, a heart with a lock and key, and a heart with a ribbon!

Abstract Heart

Let's draw a heart decorated with abstract designs.

Step 1: Draw a heart and color it in. If you want, you can add shapes and patterns to the inside of the heart, such as the small flower shown here.

Step 2: Draw a row of "humps" along one side of the heart.

Step 3: Draw a set of humps on the other side of the heart. Try to make it match the right side.

Step 4: Color in the designs you just drew.

Step 5: Draw long petal shapes at the top of the heart.

Step 6: Add a decoration to the bottom of the heart, such as this leaf with spirals on either side.

Heart Lock and Key

Who holds the key to your heart? Let's draw a heart shaped like a lock, with a key to go along with it!

Here is what the design will look like when done.

Step 1: Draw a heart.

Step 2: Draw a line to the left of your heart that follows the shape of the heart, to make it look 3-D. Color it in. Don't forget the little slanted line at the top of the heart, which gives dimension to your drawing.

Step 3: Draw the handle of the lock and color it in.

Step 4: Draw a keyhole in the middle of the heart.

Step 5: Draw an abstract design inside the heart, such as swirls like this!

Now let's draw the heart key!

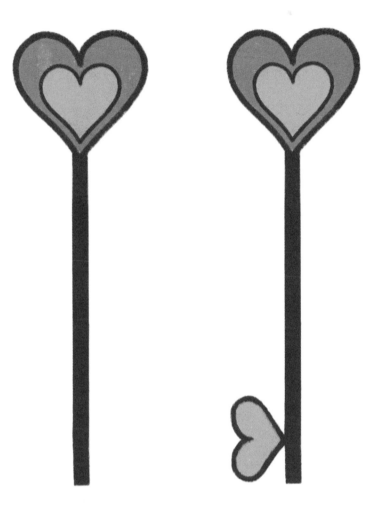

Step 6: Draw a heart, and then draw a smaller heart inside it. Color them in.

Step 7: Draw a vertical line underneath the heart.

Step 8: Draw a small heart at the bottom of the line, with the bottom of the heart touching the line.

Heart with Ribbon

Now it's time for a tattoo classic—a heart with a ribbon. You can put any word(s) you like on the ribbon, such as someone's name, your pet's name, or a phrase like "together forever" or "I love you." This version has a burst of rays behind it!

Practice this lesson on paper before you doodle it on your skin, so that you can learn how to position the edges of the ribbon and the heart in just the right place.

Step 1: Let's start by drawing the ribbon. Draw 2 parallel lines that gently curve upward, and draw 2 short lines to connect them at the ends, like you see here.

Step 2: Draw a line from the top corner that turns left and then goes up toward the right. Draw a line from the bottom corner that turns right and then goes down toward the left.

Step 3: Finish the ribbon by drawing lines that zig and then zag back toward the ribbon.

Step 4: Draw a heart behind the ribbon. It can take some practice to get the proportion of the heart just right, so practice on paper first.

Step 5: Color in the heart. You can add highlights to the top of the heart to make it look 3-D, as you see here.

Step 6: Write a word or phrase on the ribbon, and color it in.

Step 7: Optional: Draw lines around the outside of the heart to look like rays.

Doodle Your Own

Get out your markers, pens, and pencils—it's time to doodle your own mini abstract tattoos! Use these shapes and outlines as guides to create your own fun-tastic doodle tattoos.

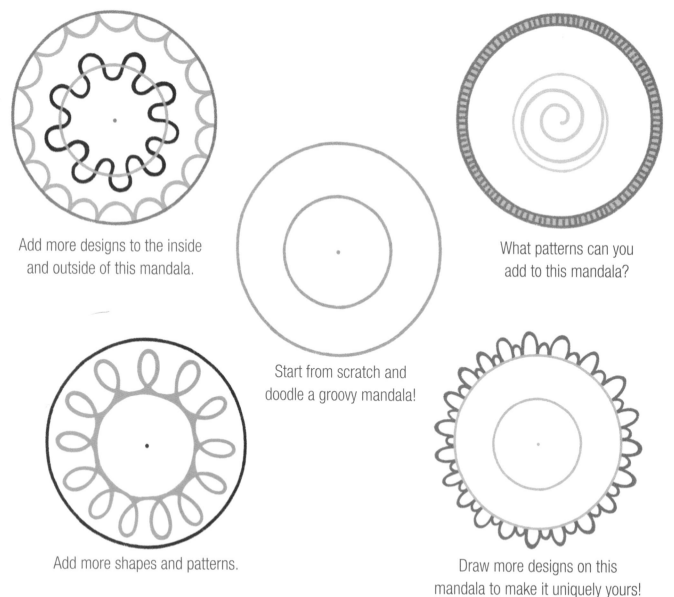

Add more designs to the inside and outside of this mandala.

Start from scratch and doodle a groovy mandala!

What patterns can you add to this mandala?

Add more shapes and patterns.

Draw more designs on this mandala to make it uniquely yours!

Draw more curved lines
connecting the star to
the end point.

Decorate this star
any way you wish!

Draw more curved
lines to finish this
shooting star. Color it in!

Add more designs to make
this a groovy heart!

Color in this heart to make it look 3-D.

Add more shapes, patterns, and
colors to this cute heart!

Doodle Mini Abstract Tattoos   73

Add patterns to the inside and outside of this paisley!

What can you add to make this paisley unique?

Add cool shapes and designs to this paisley and fill it with your favorite colors!

Finish this tulip!

Add more shape and patterns to this flower.

Chapter 3

Doodle Cute Food Tattoos

Satisfy your sweet tooth with these super-cute food doodles! Learn how to draw charming food tattoos such as cupcakes, strawberries, doughnuts, and more. Have fun with all the different toppings and decorations you can add. Be creative—why not add a butterfly to the top of your cupcake, or draw a skull on the side of your ice cream?

Cupcake

Here's an easy way to draw a cute cupcake that you can decorate in all kinds of whimsical ways! Think of all the fun toppings you can add, like sprinkles in the shapes of stars, hearts, skulls, or anything else you can imagine!

Step 1: Draw a circle, which will be your cherry. Draw a small wide U-shape at the top of the cherry, with a line coming out of it, which will be the cherry's stem.

Step 2: Draw a big pile of icing beneath the cherry. The icing almost looks like a fluffy cloud!

Step 3: Draw the baking cup by drawing a horizontal line beneath the icing, with the ends gently sloping upwards. Connect this line to the icing with a series of vertical lines.

Step 4: Add fun decorations to the icing, such as sprinkles, stars, hearts, skulls, bows, or anything else you can think of. Color it in!

Step 5: Color in the cherry and the baking cup. You can also draw patterns on the baking cup, if you like!

Strawberry

Follow these simple steps to draw a super-cute strawberry!

Step 1: Draw a shape like the one you see here, that is wide and rounded on one end and tapers to a narrow curve on the other end. This will be the main part of the strawberry.

Step 2: Draw leaves at the top of the strawberry and color them in.

Step 3: Draw the seeds of the strawberry.

Step 4: Color in the strawberry!

Doughnut

Draw a doughnut topped with delightful icing and colorful sprinkles!

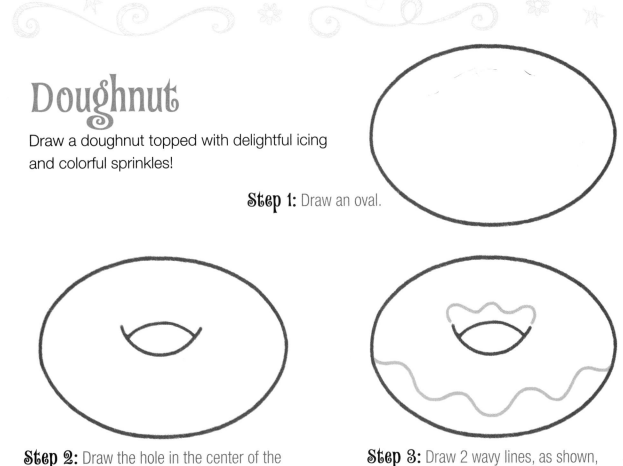

Step 1: Draw an oval.

Step 2: Draw the hole in the center of the doughnut by drawing a wide U-shape with a smaller upside-down U-shape inside of it.

Step 3: Draw 2 wavy lines, as shown, for the icing.

Step 4: Draw sprinkles on the icing.

Step 5: Color in the doughnut and the icing. Yum!

Ice Cream

Satisfy your sweet tooth by doodling a delightful ice cream cone! You can color it any way you choose and add any toppings you desire, such as sprinkles, cherries, or syrup. You can also stack several scoops of ice cream on top of the cone to create a heavenly treat!

Step 1: Draw a tall V-shape, which will be the cone.

Step 2: Draw a row of half-circles with the ends slightly curled in. This will be the bottom part of your scoop of ice cream.

Step 3: Draw a large round line connecting both sides of the drawing.

Step 4: Color in the cone and add a cherry on top.

Step 5: Draw chocolate syrup dripping on the ice cream and add sprinkles. Use fun colors!

Frozen Yogurt

Learn to draw frozen yogurt piled high in a wafer cone, covered in sprinkles!
You can also add toppings like cherries, chocolate chips, and strawberries.

Step 1: Draw 2 curved lines that meet in a point at the top. This will be the tippy top of your frozen yogurt.

Step 2: Draw a curved line on each side.

Step 3: Draw a wide curved line that connects both sides. This is your frozen yogurt!

Step 4: Draw the top of the wafer cone. (If you want to draw your frozen yogurt inside a cup instead of a cone, make this part a bit larger and skip the next step.)

Step 5: Draw the bottom part of the wafer cone.

Step 6: Draw lines inside the cone and color it in. Cover your frozen yogurt with sprinkles and color it in. You can add a cherry if you like!

Ice Cream Sundae

Learn how to draw a scrumptious ice cream sundae in a fancy glass, drizzled with chocolate syrup and topped with whipped cream and a cherry!

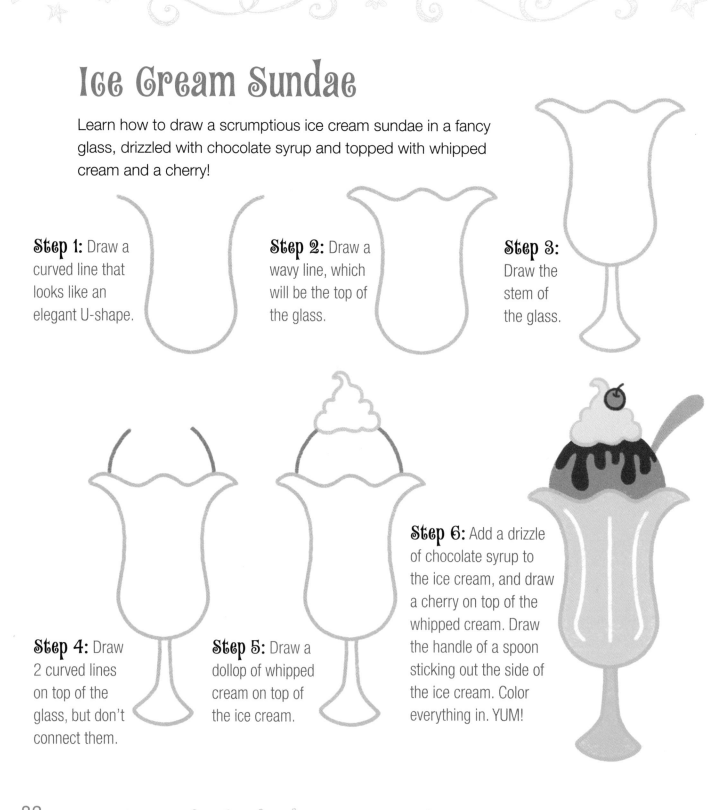

Step 1: Draw a curved line that looks like an elegant U-shape.

Step 2: Draw a wavy line, which will be the top of the glass.

Step 3: Draw the stem of the glass.

Step 4: Draw 2 curved lines on top of the glass, but don't connect them.

Step 5: Draw a dollop of whipped cream on top of the ice cream.

Step 6: Add a drizzle of chocolate syrup to the ice cream, and draw a cherry on top of the whipped cream. Draw the handle of a spoon sticking out the side of the ice cream. Color everything in. YUM!

Lollipop

Learn to draw a super-cute lollipop with a ribbon and bow. Make your lollipop as colorful as you want—the swirls are perfect for eye-popping color combinations!

Step 1: Draw a circle with a dot in the center.

Step 2: Draw a vertical line for the stick of the lollipop.

Step 3: Starting at the dot in the center of your circle, draw a swirl inside the lollipop.

Step 4: Draw curved lines inside the swirl of the lollipop.

Step 5: Color in the lollipop, using any colors you want.

Step 6: Draw 2 sideways hearts on each side of the stick, with their tips connecting. This will be your bow.

Step 7: Draw a little loop inside each half of the bow, and draw a ribbon fluttering out on each side.

Step 8: Color in the bow.

Doodle Your Own

Now it's time to experiment and doodle your own cute food tattoos! Use fun colors and add awesome details!

Draw swirls on the lollipop and a bow around the stick.

Draw the icing and toppings on this yummy cupcake!

What do you imagine will go in this bowl?

Draw icing and toppings on this delightful doughnut!

Which do prefer: ice cream or frozen yogurt? Draw it on top of this cone!

How many scoops of ice cream will you draw on top of this cone?

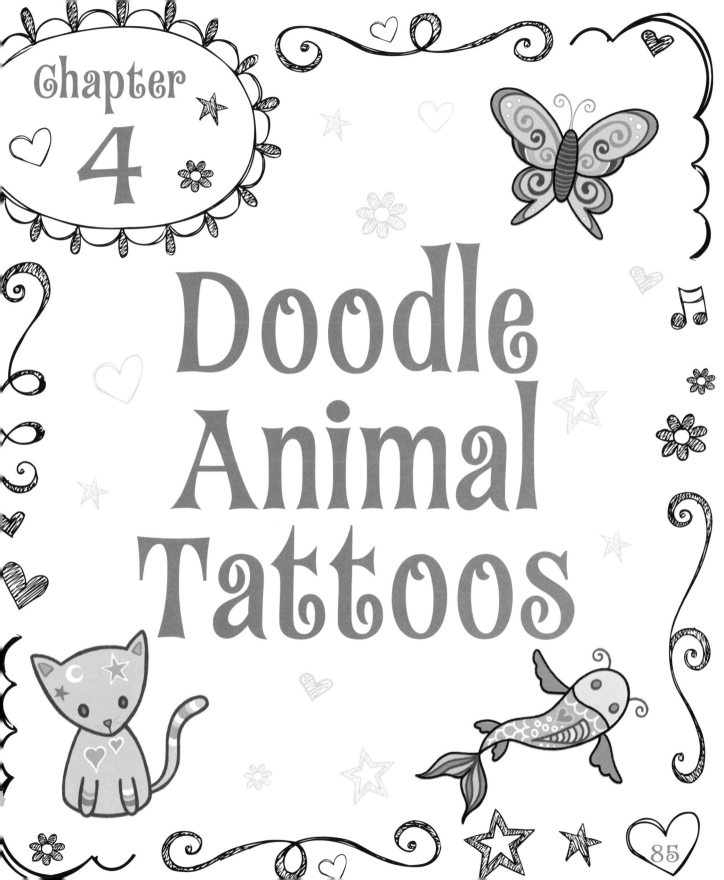

Chapter 4

Doodle Animal Tattoos

Do you love animals? Share your enthusiasm for your furry, feathered, and winged friends by drawing cute animal tattoos! Learn how to draw butterflies, cats, owls, snakes, and fish. These aren't ordinary animals—you can fill them with groovy colors and fun patterns to make them extraordinary! As usual, you don't have to follow these lessons exactly. Once you draw the basic outline of your animal, you can decorate it with the shapes and designs of your choosing, so let your imagination run wild! Above all, don't worry about making your animal tattoos look anatomically correct—just have fun with it!

Butterfly

Now let's draw a fluttery butterfly filled with shapes and patterns. Once you draw the basic outline of the butterfly, you can decorate it with any shapes, designs, and colors that you want!

Step 1: Draw a long oval for the butterfly's body, with 2 swirly lines coming out of the top for antennae.

Step 2: Draw the butterfly's top wings. Try to make them symmetrical.

Step 3: Draw the butterfly's bottom wings. Try to make them symmetrical.

Step 4: Color in the edges of the butterfly's wings.

Step 5: Draw swirls on the butterfly's top wings.

Step 6: Draw more swirls on the butterfly's wings.

Step 7: If you have room, draw more shapes and patterns on the butterfly's wings. If you run out of room, that's okay!

Step 8: Optional: Color in the rest of the butterfly.

Owl

Owls are fantastic creatures to draw because they offer lots of opportunities for detail and color. Here's how to draw a cute owl!

Step 1: Draw 2 large eyes and a "V" for a beak.

Step 2: Draw some decorations in and around the eyes, such as loops and half-circles, like you see here. You could also draw waves, spirals, dots, or anything else that makes a cute pattern around the eyes.

Step 3: Color in the eyes.

Step 4: Draw a gently curved line at the top, which will be the owl's head. Draw a wide U-shape underneath the eyes, which will be the owl's body.

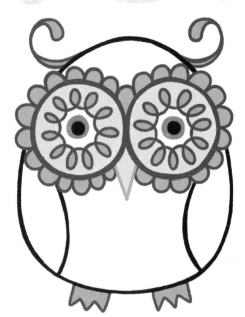

Step 5: Add decorations to the top of the owl's head, such as these curls, to represent the owl's ears. Draw a pair of feet at the bottom.

Step 6: Add shapes and designs to the owl's body, and color it in. You can draw hearts, stars, dots, peace signs, stripes, or anything else you can think of!

Step 7: Add shapes and patterns to the owl's head and wings. Let your creativity run wild to make your owl unique!

Sitting Cat

Draw a cute, cosmic kitty with her head tilted in a quizzical expression. You can decorate her fur with fun shapes and bright colors to make her totally unique! The cat's face, paws, legs, back, belly, and tail are the perfect places for pretty patterns!

Step 1: Draw a line that looks like a rounded V-shape that is slightly tilted on its side.

Step 2: Observe the shape of the line drawn here and draw a similar line to create 2 ears and the top of the cat's head.

Step 3: Draw the cat's eyes, nose, and whiskers.

Step 4: Draw the cat's body.

Step 5: Draw 2 long U-shapes for legs and feet, and a curvy line for a tail.

Step 6: Draw shapes and patterns on your kitty, and color her in!

Fish

Koi is a popular fish for tattoos because they have an elegant, flowing appearance. Here you'll learn how to draw a koi fish seen from above.

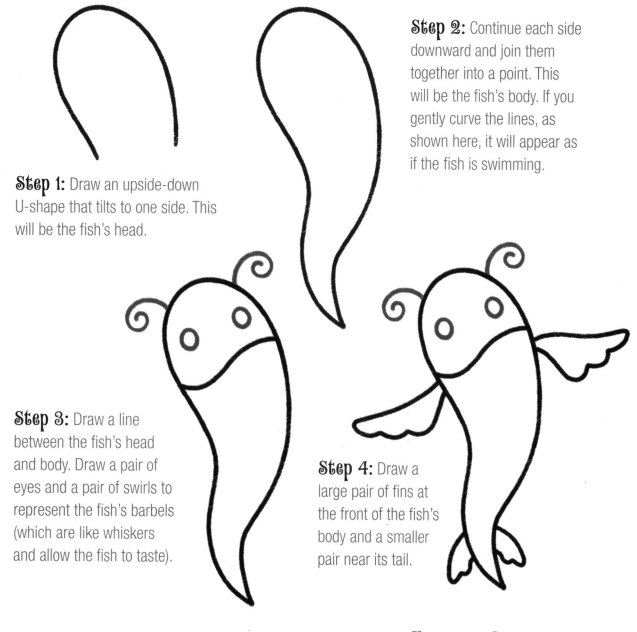

Step 2: Continue each side downward and join them together into a point. This will be the fish's body. If you gently curve the lines, as shown here, it will appear as if the fish is swimming.

Step 1: Draw an upside-down U-shape that tilts to one side. This will be the fish's head.

Step 3: Draw a line between the fish's head and body. Draw a pair of eyes and a pair of swirls to represent the fish's barbels (which are like whiskers and allow the fish to taste).

Step 4: Draw a large pair of fins at the front of the fish's body and a smaller pair near its tail.

Step 5: Draw the fish's tail.

Step 6: Draw a fin on the fish's back.

Step 7: Start coloring in the fish!

Step 8: You can add decorations to the fish's back, such as hearts, dots, stripes, or connected U-shapes that resemble scales.

Snake

The king cobra is one of the world's most venomous snakes, but you can draw it as the world's cutest snake! You can decorate your snake with fun shapes and patterns to make it as unique as you are.

Step 1: Draw a long line that curves around, up, and then down, like this. This is the snake's head and neck.

Step 2: Draw a shape that looks like a loose "6" that connects to the body, like so.

Step 3: Draw a wide curve around the snake's body, like this one. This makes it look like the snake's body is coiled.

Step 4: Draw 1 more wide curve at the bottom.

Step 5: Draw 2 curved lines on either side of the snake's head, which will be the snake's hood. Draw the snake's tail.

Step 6: Draw 2 dots for eyes and a forked flickering tongue. Draw a cute crown on the snake's head, fitting for a king cobra!

Step 7: It's fun time! Add shapes and patterns to your snake to make it really unique.

Step 8: Color in your snake using any colors you want.

Flying Cat

Let's get whimsical and draw a cat flying through the air—or even soaring through space!

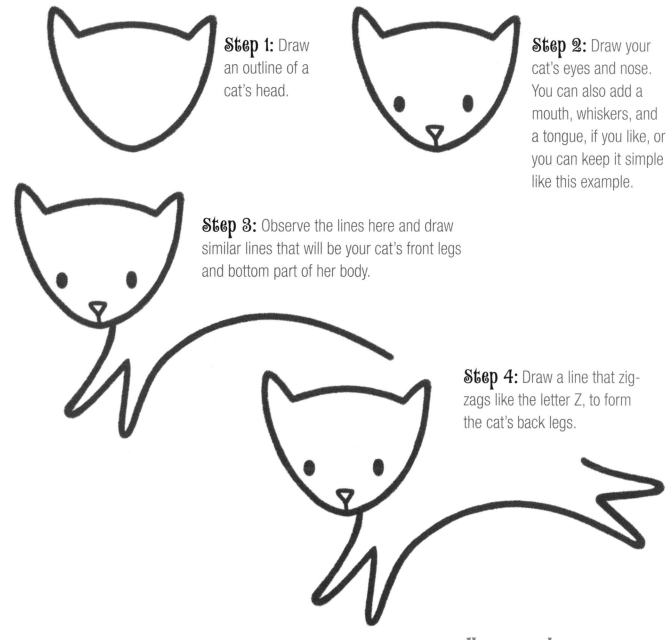

Step 1: Draw an outline of a cat's head.

Step 2: Draw your cat's eyes and nose. You can also add a mouth, whiskers, and a tongue, if you like, or you can keep it simple like this example.

Step 3: Observe the lines here and draw similar lines that will be your cat's front legs and bottom part of her body.

Step 4: Draw a line that zig-zags like the letter Z, to form the cat's back legs.

Step 5: Draw a long line that gently curves upward and then back, to form the cat's back and tail.

Step 6: Draw the cat a scarf or cape that flaps in the wind! Draw shapes and patterns on the cat and surround her with stars or other images, like flowers or rainbows.

Step 7: Draw more shapes and patterns if you wish, and color it in!

Doodle Your Own

Now it's your turn! Finish these animal outlines to make them your own. Add shapes, patterns, and designs using any colors you want. Have fun with it!

Give this kitty a face and body.

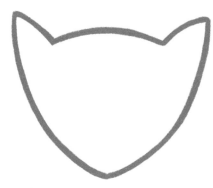

Draw this cat a body and color it in!

Finish the snake by adding more coils and a tail, plus color it in with designs!

Draw fins on the fish and color it in!

Add antennae, and draw fun shapes on the butterfly's wings!

Fill the butterfly's wings with groovy patterns and color it in.

Give this owl wings and ears. Fill his feathers with fun designs and colors!

Chapter 5

Doodle Sugar Skull Tattoos

Sugar skulls are colorful candy gifts that are given on Mexico's famous holiday, Day of the Dead (or *Día de los Muertos* in Spanish). The holiday is becoming more and more popular in the United States and all around the world, as people connect with the holiday's special meaning of honoring and celebrating our loved ones who have passed away. It's not a sad holiday, but a festive one full of colorful imagery and meaningful traditions.

Sugar skulls are super fun to draw because once you draw the basic skull outline, you can decorate them with any shapes, colors, or patterns that you want! You can draw sugar skulls to reflect your personality or to honor someone you love.

How to Draw a Skull

Step 1: Draw a circle. It doesn't have to be a perfect circle—imperfection adds personality!

Step 2: Draw 2 circles inside the large circle, for the skull's eyes. Draw them on the mid to lower half of the big circle.

Step 3: Draw an upside-down heart for the skull's nose.

Step 4: Draw a wide U-shape beneath the big circle. This will be the skull's jaw.

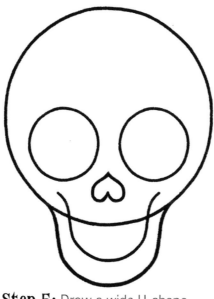

Step 5: Draw a wide U-shape, which will be the outline of the skull's mouth.

Step 6: Draw the skull's teeth.

Sugar Skulls

It's time to turn your skull outlines into spectacular sugar skulls by filling them in with groovy shapes, patterns, and colors! Remember, you don't need to follow these steps exactly. There is a lot of room for creativity, so let loose and have fun!

Sugar Skull with Flowery Eyes

This first sugar skull is decorated with large flower eyes that'll make you think of spring.

Step 1: Draw a skull as described earlier in this chapter.

Step 2: Draw flowers inside the eye sockets and color them in.

Step 3: Draw a row of half-circles around the outer edge of the eyes.

Step 4: Draw a flower in the center of the skull's forehead, and a small petal shape beneath it.

Step 5: Draw designs on the sides of the skull, such as these flowers with swirls in between each petal.

Step 6: Fill in the empty spaces with simple shapes like dots or half-circles.

Step 7: Draw designs above the skull's mouth and on the skull's jaw.

Sugar Skull with Heart Eyes

Here's a sugar skull that symbolizes love.

Step 1: Draw a skull as described earlier in this chapter. Color in the nose and teeth, and draw a heart inside each eye.

Step 2: Draw a pattern around the skull's eyes, such as these pointy waves.

Step 3: Draw a paisley on the skull's forehead. Fill it with shapes and designs, and color it in.

Step 4: Draw more paisley shapes on the forehead. Try to draw the paisley from different angles, for variety.

Step 5: Draw shapes and designs inside the paisleys, and color them in.

Step 6: Fill in the empty spaces with shapes like circles, flowers, stars, or anything else you can think of.

Step 7: Draw designs around the skull's mouth, such as a mustache, flowers, and petal shapes.

Sugar Skull with Peace Signs

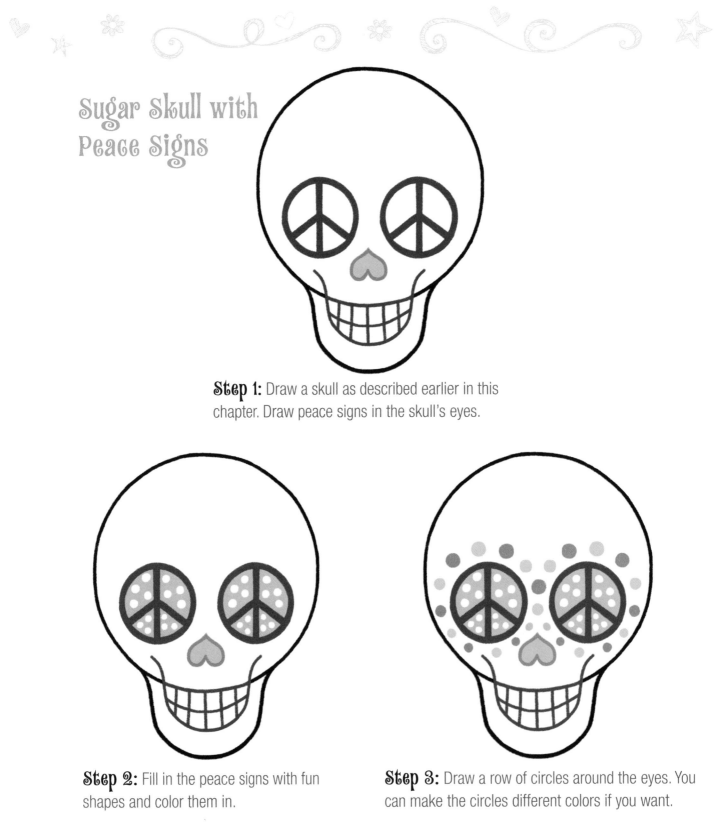

Step 1: Draw a skull as described earlier in this chapter. Draw peace signs in the skull's eyes.

Step 2: Fill in the peace signs with fun shapes and color them in.

Step 3: Draw a row of circles around the eyes. You can make the circles different colors if you want.

Step 4: Draw pointy petals on the very top of the skull's head, and color the inside of the petals with designs like these loopy lines.

Step 5: Add a row of half-circles along the outer edge of the pointy petals.

Step 6: Fill in the extra space on the forehead with flowers and dots.

Step 7: Draw flowers and dots around the skull's mouth.

Sugar Skull with Butterfly

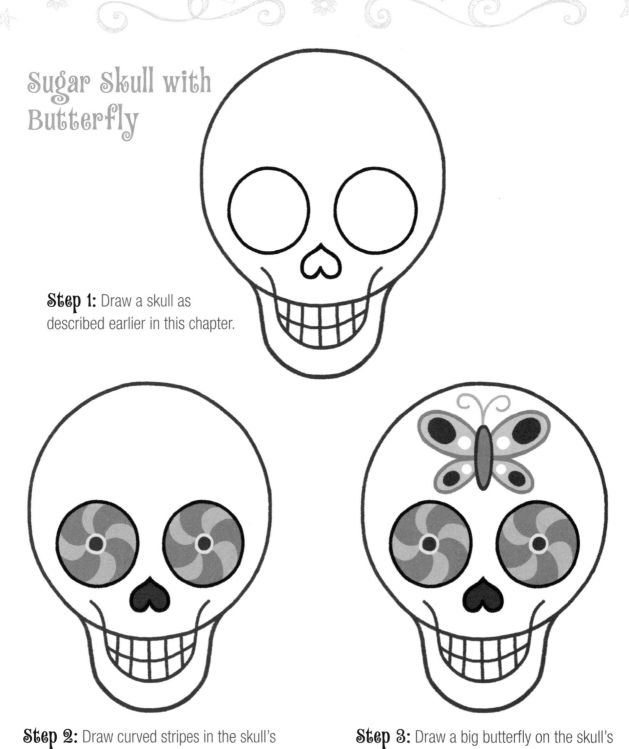

Step 1: Draw a skull as described earlier in this chapter.

Step 2: Draw curved stripes in the skull's eye sockets, and color them in. Color in the skull's nose.

Step 3: Draw a big butterfly on the skull's forehead.

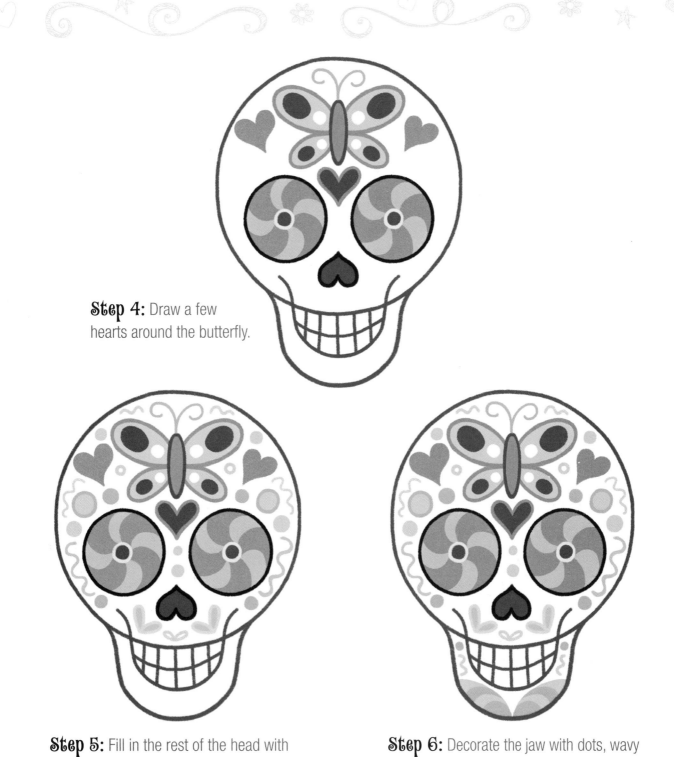

Step 4: Draw a few hearts around the butterfly.

Step 5: Fill in the rest of the head with more shapes, such as circles, dots, wavy lines, and petal shapes.

Step 6: Decorate the jaw with dots, wavy lines, and curved stripes.

Doodle Your Own

Now it's your turn to doodle smiling skulls and turn them into sugar skulls! Think of all the cool shapes and patterns you can draw on the skulls. Use lots of color!

Finish this skull by adding a jaw, teeth, and a nose.

What shapes and patterns can you add to this sugar skull?

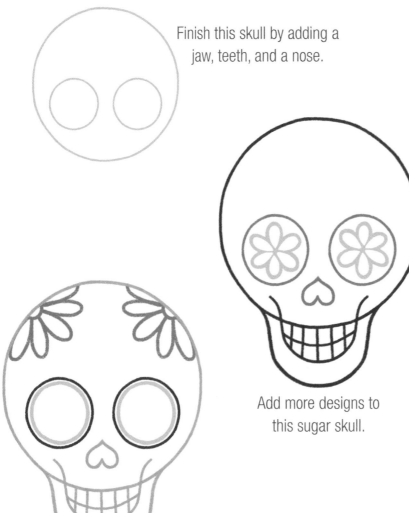

Add more designs to this sugar skull.

Add shapes and designs to make this sugar skull unique!

Decorate this skull with fun shapes and colors!

Chapter 6

Doodle Henna Tattoo Designs

Your hands are the perfect place for drawing pretty patterns. Learn how to turn your fingers, palms, and wrists into whimsical works of art!

Many cultures around the world create dye from a plant called henna, which is used to draw intricate designs on hands, arms, and feet. Henna is an ancient form of temporary tattooing, and the designs are just as stylish today.

Get inspired by this age-old art form and create your own henna tattoo designs! You can decorate your hands with fun swirly designs, abstract patterns, pretty flowers . . . and anything else you want!

Should you draw on the top of your hand or the underside of your hand? It's up to you! One thing to keep in mind is that the design will probably last longer on the top of your hand, because the palm of your hand can get sweaty or the design may rub off your fingers when you touch things.

First you'll learn how to draw designs on your fingers, and then your palm, and then your wrist . . . and then it's time to put it all together!

Fingers

The patterns on your fingers will go from your fingertip to the base of your palm. You can draw the same pattern on each finger, or draw a different pattern per finger, whichever you prefer. You can also draw a special image on your fingertip—like a flower, star, or peace sign—it doesn't necessarily need to be part of the pattern on the rest of your finger.

Finger A

Step 1: Draw a wavy line with a little loop at the bottom and a swirl at the fingertip.

Step 2: Draw half-circles inside the waves on one side of the design.

Step 3: Draw circles inside the waves on the other side. You can also draw stars, hearts, or flowers!

Finger B

Step 1: Draw flowers on your finger, leaving space in between each flower.

Step 2: Draw a little sun in between each flower.

Step 3: Color in the flowers and suns!

Finger 6

Step 1: At the base of your finger, draw a line that points up in the center, like this.

Step 2: Draw petal shapes below the line you just drew.

Step 3: Draw swirls from the tip of the point to the top of your finger.

Step 4: Add more decorations, like these dots.

Palm

The palm of your hand is a fun place to draw something that expresses your personality, whether it's a mandala, a heart, a peace sign, butterflies, or any other image that makes you happy, like your favorite pet or a symbol of your favorite hobby. The possibilities are endless! You don't have to worry about drawing anything realistic because henna designs are meant to be abstract, so just have fun with it!

You can draw an image in the center of your palm, or you can draw images all across your palm. Your image can be symmetrical or asymmetrical, it's up to you!

Mandala Flower Palm

Step 1: Draw a circle in the middle of your palm, and draw another circle around that.

Step 2: Draw petals around the circle to make a flower.

Step 3: Add more petal shapes and dots around the outside of the flower.

Step 4: Color it in!

Peace Sign Palm

Step 1: Draw a peace sign in the center of your palm.

Step 2: Color the inside of the peace sign.

Step 3: Draw small petals around the outside of the peace sign.

Step 4: Draw large petals around the outside of the peace sign.

Step 5: Color it in!

Butterfly Garden Palm

Step 1: Draw a few butterflies on your palm.

Step 2: Decorate the butterflies' wings with circles, flowers, loops, stars, or any other shapes you like.

Step 3: Finish decorating the butterflies and color them in.

Step 4: Draw swirls in between the butterflies. Try to fill in all the spaces around the butterflies all the way to the edge of your palm. You can carry on the swirls to the other side of your hand, too!

Wrist

The designs on your wrist will go from one side to the other, kind of like a groovy bracelet. You can draw a pattern that goes all the way across, or you can draw a single image in the middle of your wrist (such as a butterfly, heart, peace sign, etc.) with symmetrical designs on either side. Have fun with it!

Loopy Wrist Pattern

Step 1: Draw a loopy line across your wrist.

Step 2: Draw a wavy line underneath the loopy line, echoing the same shape as above.

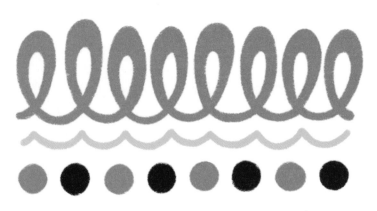

Step 3: Draw a row of circles underneath the lines.

Flower Wrist Design

Step 1: Draw a wavy line across your wrist.

Step 2: Draw flowers on the top "humps" of the wave.

Step 3: Draw curved lines in the bottom parts of the wave, and lines under the bottom "humps" of the wave.

Butterfly Wrist Design

Step 1: Draw a butterfly in the center of your wrist.

Step 2: Draw decorative details on the butterfly's wings.

Step 3: Color in the butterfly.

Step 4: Draw swirls on each side of the butterfly. Try to make them symmetrical.

Put It All Together

Now you're ready to draw henna designs all over your hand! Here's how it looks when you combine the designs you learned in the previous lessons for fingers, wrists, and palms.

Mandala Hand

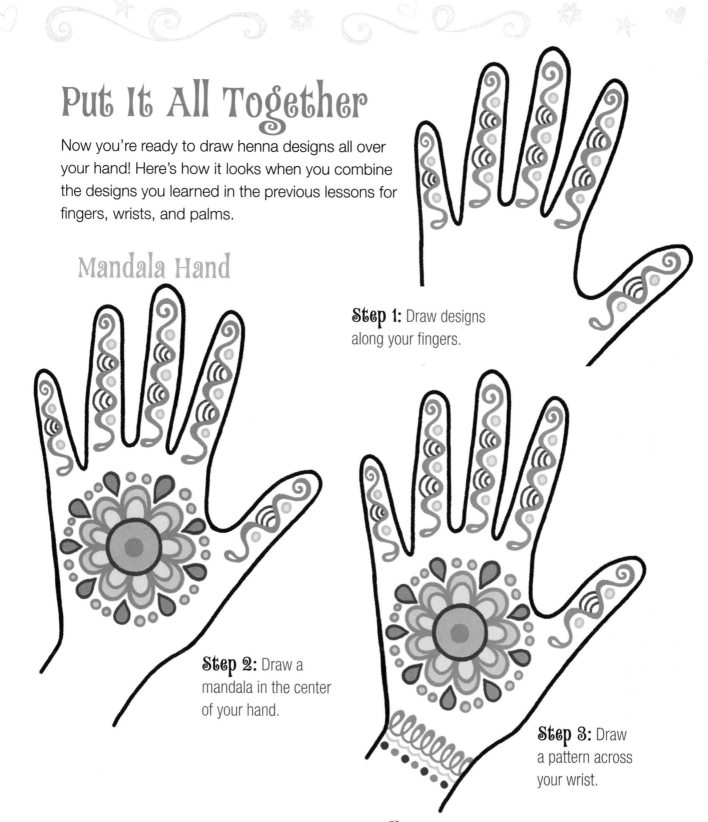

Step 1: Draw designs along your fingers.

Step 2: Draw a mandala in the center of your hand.

Step 3: Draw a pattern across your wrist.

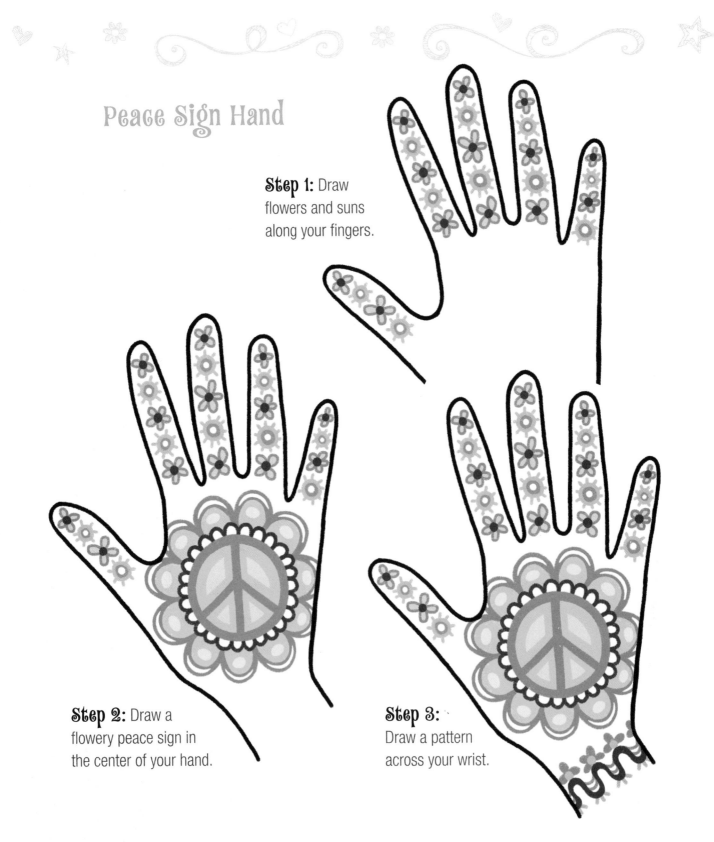

Peace Sign Hand

Step 1: Draw flowers and suns along your fingers.

Step 2: Draw a flowery peace sign in the center of your hand.

Step 3: Draw a pattern across your wrist.

Butterfly Hand

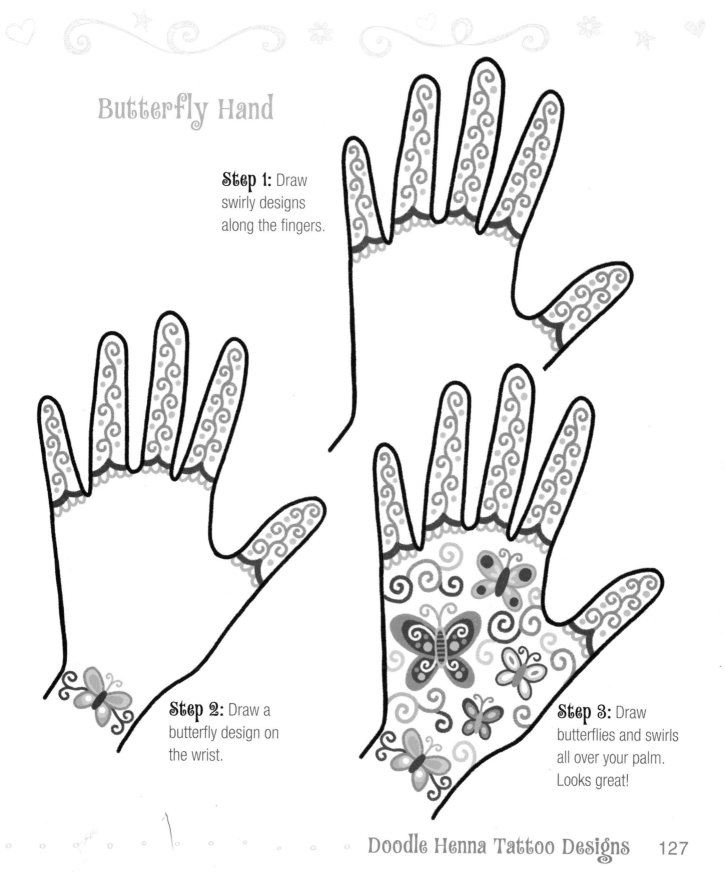

Step 1: Draw swirly designs along the fingers.

Step 2: Draw a butterfly design on the wrist.

Step 3: Draw butterflies and swirls all over your palm. Looks great!

Doodle Your Own

What designs can you come up with? Practice doodling henna hand designs on these hand outlines. Draw on the fingers, palms, and wrists using any colors you want!

Finish this henna hand design!

Fill this hand with fun patterns using the designs here as a starting point!

Now it's time to start your henna designs from scratch!